TEACHER'S RESOURCE BOOK

Copyright © by Harcourt, Inc.

All rights reserved. No part of this publication may be reproduced or transmitted in any form or by any means, electronic or mechanical, including photocopy, recording, or any information storage and retrieval system, without permission in writing from the publisher.

Permission is hereby granted to individual teachers using the corresponding student's textbook or kit as the major vehicle for regular classroom instruction to photocopy complete pages from this publication in classroom quantities for instructional use and not for resale. Requests for information on other matters regarding duplication of this work should be addressed to School Permissions and Copyrights, Harcourt, Inc., 6277 Sea Harbor Drive, Orlando, Florida 32887-6777. Fax: 407-345-2418.

HARCOURT and the Harcourt Logo are trademarks of Harcourt, Inc., registered in the United States of America and/or other jurisdictions.

Printed in the United States of America

ISBN 0-15-335212-4

2 3 4 5 6 7 8 9 10   073   10 09 08 07 06 05 04 03 02

Orlando   Austin   Chicago   New York   Toronto   London   San Diego

Visit The Learning Site!
www.harcourtschool.com

Contents

The High-Frequency Word Cards are alphabetized in two sections: short words and long words. Long words are five letters or more and begin on page 65.

High-Frequency Word Cards .... Pages 1–114

Lesson 1: *am, jump, run, walk*

Lesson 2: *look*

Lesson 3: *big, funny, just*

Lesson 4: *finds, friend, on, where*

Lesson 5: *down, up*

Lesson 7: *oh, play*

Lesson 8: *began, good, help, took, when*

Lesson 9: *everybody*

Lesson 10: *good*

Lesson 11: *everyone, home, who*

Lesson 12: *couldn't, into, out, saw*

Lesson 13: *by, says, should, today, two*

Lesson 14: *about, made, wanted*

Lesson 15: *fly, four, gave, three, time, very*

Lesson 16: *different, eat, even, lives, sometimes*

Lesson 17: *every, give, how, make, needs, our, own, their*

Lesson 18: *goes, name, new, over, sea, use, very*

Lesson 19: *sleep, try*

Lesson 20: *thought, world*

Lesson 21: *book, food, mother, right*

Lesson 22: *brought, shared, something, story, write*

Lesson 23: *children, soon, through, town, under*

Lesson 24: *ago, air, another, around, eyes, maybe, watched*

Lesson 25: *blue, found, from, many, water*

Lesson 26: *floor, laugh, love, opened, people, pretty*

Lesson 27: *away, cook, door, even, only*

Lesson 28: *been, know, picture, sure*

Lesson 29: *always, beautiful, brothers, nothing, school, together*

Lesson 30: *couldn't, knew*

Punctuation Cards .... Page 63

Posters
High-Frequency Hugo .... Page 115
Phonics Phyllis .... Page 117
Reading Rosa .... Page 119
Fluency Felix .... Page 121

Grouping Chart .... Page 123

Story Wheel .... Page 125

ago

air

Grade 1 • Teacher's Resource Book

Ago

Air

am

away

Am

Away

been

big

Been

Big

blue

book

Blue

Book

by

cook

By

Cook

door

down

Door

Down

eat

even

Eat

Even

eyes

fly

Eyes

Fly

food

four

Food

Four

from

gave

From

Gave

give

goes

Give

Goes

good

help

Good

Help

home

how

Home

How

into

jump

Into

Jump

just

knew

Just

Knew

know

look

Know

Look

love

made

Love

Made

make

many

Make

Many

name

new

Name

New

oh

on

Oh

On

only

our

Only

Our

out

over

Out

Over

own

play

Own

Play

run

saw

Run

Saw

says

sea

Says

Sea

soon

sure

Soon

Sure

time

took

Time

Took

town

try

Town

Try

two

up

Two

Up

use

very

Use

Very

walk

when

Walk

When

who

. ? !

Grade 1 • Teacher's Resource Book

Who

, 's

about

always

About

Always

another

around

Around

Another

Teacher's Resource Book • Grade 1

beautiful

began

Began

Beautiful

brothers

brought

Brought

Brothers

72 Teacher's Resource Book • Grade 1

children

couldn't

Children

Couldn't

different

every

Grade 1 • Teacher's Resource Book

Different

Every

everybody

everyone

Everyone

Everybody

finds

floor

Floor

Finds

Teacher's Resource Book • Grade 1

found

friend

Found

Friend

funny

laugh

Laugh

Funny

lives

maybe

Maybe

Lives

mother

needs

Mother

Needs

nothing

opened

Opened

Nothing

people

picture

Picture

People

pretty

right

Grade 1 • Teacher's Resource Book

Pretty

Right

school

shared

Shared

school

should

sleep

sleep

should

something

sometimes

sometimes

something

story

their

Their

Story

thought

three

Three

Thought

through

today

Today

Through

together

under

Together

Under

wanted

watched

watched

wanted

water

where

Water

Where

112 Teacher's Resource Book • Grade 1

world

write

Write

World

High-Frequency Hugo

Phonics Phyllis

Reading Rosa

Fluency Felix

Grouping Chart

GROUP 1	GROUP 2	GROUP 3
With Teacher	Centers	At My Desk/ Practice Pages
At My Desk/ Practice Pages	With Teacher	Centers
Centers	At My Desk/ Practice Pages	With Teacher

Story Wheel

Cut out the spinner and glue it to tagboard. In the center, insert a brad, using it to attach a large paper-clip "pointer." Have children spin the pointer to tell about: characters, the setting, how they felt about the story, and their favorite part of the story.

Grade 1 • Teacher's Resource Book